Principles Of Promotion

Winning Career Strategies

That Get You Promoted

Time and Time Again

ANDREA D. ODEN

Copyright © 2019 Andrea D. Oden

ISBN: 978-1-0798-0357-0

FOR THE LAST TWENTY YEARS, I have had the extraordinary privilege of working alongside some of the most capable leaders in both Corporate America and in the Kingdom of God. I've worked with CEOs, Vice Presidents, Directors, Managers and Supervisors who have all taught me some truly great lesson about leadership. I've also had the honor to serve, sit at the feet of and learn from some of the world's greatest pastors, teachers and church staff members. It has been my pleasure to work within the telecommunications industry growing leaders and working with some of the brightest in the business. You have no idea how much you all have taught me about serving and leading with a loving heart.

This book is from my heart to yours, with great love and admiration!

For Kayla,

Everything I am and all that I do is for you. You are my greatest joy, the song I sing. You are the very beat of my heart. It is my honor and pleasure to be your mother

Table of Contents

Acknowledgments

There are people in our lives whose encouragement, partnership and support make not only our careers but our dreams possible!

To all the teams that I have had the pleasure of partnering with over the last twenty years, you have helped make this book possible.

To my tribe – those who have allowed me into your lives and careers, it has been my honor to coach, mentor, encourage and to serve you. You have made me dream bigger, and so much better.

Lastly, to the John Maxwell Team, you have pushed me beyond my comfort zone only to discover a greatness I never knew. I am humbled and deeply honored to be part of this great team.

Introduction

"What does a person have to do to get promoted around here?"
"I've been here for years. Everybody's getting promoted except me."
"Who do you have to kiss up to if you want to get ahead?"
"Maybe I should just quit. People just don't like me."
"I do everything they tell me to do and every time a manager role comes up, I don't get it."

These are the phrases I hear time and time again. People want to know how to move forward, how to grow in their career. Everyone wants to know how to get promoted.

Do any of these phrases sound familiar to you? Have you said similar things? I know I have.

I've had many "jobs" over my lifetime. In my twenties, I went with whatever life happened to throw my way. I was a receptionist, I sold cosmetics and I was a word processor. Between the ages of twenty and twenty-nine, I had eleven jobs with eleven different companies. Around this time, I realized that there were people out there who had careers they loved, and were making hundreds of thousands of dollars doing what they loved every day. In my thirties, I was a pastor of a church where I learned my hardest leadership lessons. I learned so much about people and leadership. In my late thirties, I fell into a career in Human Resources. It started with a contract assignment as a secretary, and at the time of writing this book has turned into a fifteen-year love affair – a dream career.

Being a director of human resources doesn't always make for a very glamorous day at work. During my early years in human resources, the only time I sat across the desk from an employee was to discipline them, help them go out of the business on a leave of absence or to terminate their employment. Today, I have very different conversations with employees. I teach leadership to everyone I encounter, no matter what their title. Long before an employee is being disciplined or facing termination, they typically have had conversations with me about their goals, their purpose and how to get there. Over the last ten years, I've practiced a few simple principles that have helped me get to the next level in my career. About five years ago, I began sharing these principles with individuals all over the United States, and I've seen people get promoted as well as find joy and great pleasure in their work.

There was a time when I was just like you. I didn't know what to do to get promoted. I tried to do what others did. I tried to impersonate others within the company. I mimicked the loudest person in the room, the person I thought had the most power. I took classes, got a new wardrobe. Nothing seemed to work. Then I got strategic. I started putting a few simple principles into place and amazingly, opportunities started coming my way. I was getting promoted not only at the company I worked for, but other organizations started reaching out to me also. When I became a leadership coach, I tested these principles on my clients and a few friends. Each time, promotional opportunities came. Do I have the secret to promotion? Have I uncovered the principles to success? I believe I have. And I call them the **Principles of Promotion.**

I have put these principles into what I believe is a structured approach. However, please feel free to dive in as you like. Each chapter requires less than a one-hour reading commitment on your part but will hopefully serve you for a lifetime – a lifetime of a joyful career that brings out your best passions and sets you on a path for promotion time and time again. My recommendation is that you go through this book principle by principle in their exact order. Take a week and focus on each principle. Discuss it with some friends. Apply the principle strategies at the end of each chapter. Make a conscience decision to incorporate what you're learning into your daily routine. You will be surprised at how much you will learn and grow over the course of a few short months.

The Mirror Principle

"You learn more in failure than you ever do in success."

~ Jay-Z

What mistakes have I made? What am I pretending not to know? What could I have done differently? What am I doing to dishonor myself and others?

These are all questions I've had to ask myself. Years ago, I found myself at a cross roads. I felt like Bill Murray's character in the movie Groundhog Day. I kept replaying the same career moves over and over. Year after year, I would do the same thing. Between the ages of twenty and twenty-nine, I held eleven different positions with eleven different companies. Following this extended job tour, I finally settled down and decided to stay with one organization. I worked really hard. I loved my boss, she was truly great to work for. She got promoted and I thought she would take me with her, but she didn't. When she didn't offer me to go with her, I was sure I'd get to replace her. The role opened and everyone said I was a shoe-in, as I often filled in for her when she was traveling or on vacation. I was the likely choice. I bought a new power suit and had a great interview. I was counting my new paycheck; but I didn't get the job. They actually rehired someone who had quit the company a few years previous. They relocated her and her family from Colorado and I ended up training her. I was angry for a long time. I was angry with my boss, I felt like she could have done more for me. I had worked my butt off for her. Why didn't she look out for me? Then I became angry with my new boss. I was way smarter than she was. Every day she would ask me questions about how to do her job. I was angry with the company. How could they rehire someone who had already quit? Why would they spend all that money to relocate someone when I was sitting right there already doing the damn job? I eventually left for a new position with another company. I stayed there for about a year, but I hated it. While I was on maternity leave, I found a new job. I worked there for two years until I was let go during a downsizing of the company, shortly after the 9/11 tragedies.

I received a really great severance package and I didn't work for six months. I decided to just relax. I thought about starting my own business – again. The thought didn't last very long. During this time, I did do a lot of thinking, and as I did a lot of soul searching, I discovered that I was the problem.

The Mirror Principle is the starting principle within the Principles of Promotion, where you take a hard, honest look at yourself. You look at all the things you did wrong. Not what they did to you, not how unfair it was, but you look at yourself. You hold a mirror up to your face and you deal with the mistakes you've made. My mistakes were many. In my twenties, I had a major attendance problem. I was creative and very smart, but I was not dependable. My boss never knew when I'd show up and because I had a job every year for years, nobody knew when I'd come in and submit my well-used resignation letter. While my boss really liked me, she knew she couldn't take me with her to her new team because I was often late to work. I thought she didn't mind because she'd stopped mentioning it. At first, she would reprimand me for being late. After a while she stopped talking about it all together. I thought we had an "understanding." She liked me and I did such great work, I thought she was "letting me slide." In fact, she didn't care because her promotion had been in the works for months and she knew I'd eventually be someone else's problem.

By the time I got to the next company, I was so angry I did just the bare minimum. I came in, still not on time most days, did just what was required of me and I left. I had a new baby at home, and I didn't care enough to do anything extra. When the company began downsizing after 9/11, I was one of the first to go. So here are my answers to the questions.

What mistakes had I made? I had an attendance problem that I never solved. I spent years not showing up to work on time. When someone finally called me on it, I'd quit and find another job. When I finally found a position I really enjoyed, I continued the behavior and pretended not to notice that my boss indeed did care about me being late. I dishonored my boss and our friendship by not committing to being at work and being on time every day. I could have done things a lot differently. I should have been punctual. I could have been more respectful of my boss, the company and myself. I spent a lot of years starting over at the bottom of a lot of companies because I couldn't admit my own mistakes. When I finally looked back, I realized that I'd wasted about fifteen years starting over when I could have grown with an organization. Today, I coach leaders and the first place we start is in the mirror. So that's where we will start. When you think of your career, when you think of the times you've been passed over for promotion, what does the mirror reveal?

The principle of the mirror is hard. It puts all the blame on you. You cannot change other people, but you can change you. We've all made mistakes that have hindered or halted our careers. We've all stayed too long at the proverbial "ball". We've blamed our bosses, our team members and anyone we can. When in reality, the fault lies with the person in the mirror. No one can stop your promotion. No one can prevent you from advancing within the organization. The only person to blame for you not moving forward in your career is you. Take your power back today and let's start moving forward. Own the mistakes you've made so that you will never make them again. We look in the mirror, but we don't stay there. We look in the mirror to face ourselves, and then we get busy doing the work required to move forward. We get busy doing the work of being better versions of ourselves.

When you're really ready for your next promotion, or you're challenged with why you're not getting promotional opportunities, start by asking yourself these four questions. No excuses, just the truth. This is by far the most difficult principle. It gets a lot easier from here. I promise!

Applying the Mirror Principle

Answer the following Mirror Reflection Questions:

- When you think of your current or last role, what mistakes have you made?

- What are you pretending not to know about where you are in your career?

- What could you have done differently?

- What are you doing to dishonor yourself or others?

Now take a deep breath, get out of that mirror and let's get moving!

The Attitude Principle

Happiness is an attitude. We either make ourselves miserable, or happy and strong. The amount of work is the same.

~Francesca Reigler

When it's time for promotion, most top-level leaders care more about your attitude than they do your skills. While writing this book, I asked thirty leaders starting at the Director level all the way up through CEO what they looked for most when promoting from within the company. Hands down, each one quickly talked about attitude. For most of these leaders, attitude came before skill set. A Vice President of a major healthcare firm said it very simply, "Andrea, I can teach skills. I can pay for training, but you can't teach attitude." Let's be honest, nobody wants to spend eight hours a day with someone with a bad attitude. The attitude principle is about your attitude in three key areas:

Your Attitude Towards People – It is important to have a positive and helpful attitude towards people. Do you have a genuine willingness to help others? Do others like working with you? Do you like working with others? Whether this means being helpful to clients/customers or to your coworkers, great leaders can be counted on to jump in and help whoever, whenever needed. This also means respecting everyone at every level. How you treat the person who cleans the restrooms is equally as important as how you treat the Vice President. Earlier this year, I was coaching a client who had just accepted a position as a manager. While she had been a manager at a much smaller firm, this would be her first time managing a large team within a large company. When she arrived on her first day, she discovered there had been a flood in her office and she had to sit in a cubicle area, on another floor, where employees who took incoming customer calls sat. She spent about four weeks sitting with these employees and they all assumed she did the same job because she sat there. She quickly made friends and learned a lot about the department and the organization without ever telling anyone her role. The day before she would move into her newly remodeled office, she was on the phone at her temporary desk when a large man walked over and dropped his backpack and coffee on her desk. The man sat on the edge of the desk with his back to her and took a personal phone call from his cell phone. Shocked, she cleared her throat and he smirked and again turned his back still laughing and talking loudly on his cell phone. She placed her call on hold and stared at him in disbelief. The man finished his call just as another woman walked up and asked him what he was doing. He flipped his hand in dismissal at my client, telling the woman that she was just an agent and not important. Fast forward, about two months later, the same man found himself in my client's office interviewing for one of her open leadership positions. She said you could have bought him with a dime. The moment he saw her, he realized his mistake and hung his head in shame. How you treat people matters. Your attitude towards people, at all levels, matters. By the way, he didn't get the job!

Your Attitude Towards the Company – Why is it that there are people who work for the same company but have different attitudes about the company? I once had the pleasure of working with a very sweet older woman. When I met her, she'd been with the company for over thirty-five years. She'd been promoted just twice in her career and absolutely loved what she did – which, by the way, was the Executive Assistant to the Sr. Vice President. Marge was a delightful woman. Everybody loved Marge and Marge loved everybody, except one person. Marge couldn't stand Denise and it was quite obvious that Denise didn't like Marge either. One day while I was talking with Marge, I asked her about her dislike of Denise. She told me she didn't like Denise because Denise hated the company. Marge went on to tell me that every day Denise had something negative to say about the company, the leaders, the policies and even the bathroom paper towels. Marge wished Denise would just get another job if she hated the company so much. A short time later, I asked Denise about Marge. Denise's response was slightly different. Denise said she disliked Marge because Marge acted like she ran the company. According to Denise, Marge was always telling people what to do and how to do it. Marge couldn't see that the attendance policy wasn't fair, and they all needed more vacation time. In Denise's opinion, Marge was just another company suck up and did everything that anybody told her to do. Denise had been with the company for about four years and she was just waiting for Marge to retire so, in her words, "I can show these blue suits what I can do."

Denise never did get to show the "blue suits" what she could do, because she was fired less than a year later. Marge eventually did retire. When she retired, her boss rented a huge banquet hall and gave her a party that peopled talked about for years to come. My question to you is, are you a Marge or a Denise? When you talk about the company, what is your attitude like? If you have a bad attitude towards the company, how can the company not have a bad attitude about you? It's like inviting people into your home for dinner and you spend the entire time talking about how much you hate your house and your family. How can you expect to get promoted at a company you dislike?

Your Attitude Towards Change – Successful companies are in the business of making money. When the company stops making money, the business ends and so do jobs. If you are planning to remain employed with a company for several years, you have to get used to change. If nothing ever changes, the company will go out of business (ask the former employees of Blockbuster Videos, Nokia or MySpace). Your attitude towards change has to be one of flexibility and resilience. When key leaders are looking to promote, they are watching your attitude when business needs change. They are watching how you handle challenges. When opportunities arise, are you able to quickly shift gears and move forward, or are you griping and complaining? A positive attitude towards change requires resilience. Resilience is your ability to effectively respond to the pressures and changes at work. When you have a resilient attitude, others see you as having the ability to deal with new and changing demands that are placed on you. In short, people see you changing and growing into the next level of leadership. They see you easily adapting to your new promotion and able to handle anything that comes your way.

A positive attitude enables you to enjoy your work and also helps others enjoy working with you. To sum up the Attitude Principle: you choose your attitude. No matter what happens, you get to choose your response.

Every day, you get to choose your attitude. Choose wisely.

Applying the Attitude Principle

When it comes to your attitude, answer the following questions:

- In what ways have you shown a genuine willingness to help others?

- In what ways can you tell others enjoy working with you?

- What is the vision for your company and/or department?

- What are some positive things you've said about the organization in the last twelve months?

- How have you shown resilience to your leaders when changes arise?

- In what ways are you known for displaying a positive attitude?

- List three to five action steps you can take to you improve your attitude.

The Brand Principle

Brand yourself for the career you want, not the job you have.

~ Dan Schawbel.

Think back to your first day on the job. You were excited, anxious and probably a little nervous. One thing is for sure, you were in love with idea of your new company. You had high hopes for the endless possibilities and opportunities. I would be willing to bet a recruiter or a hiring manager told you stories of people within the company who had been promoted time and time again. There were people in the company who started at an entry-level position and are now managers, directors and even vice presidents. You were on the yellow brick road to success. Now fast forward to today – that yellow brick road did not lead to the magic land of career gold. It didn't lead you to the land flowing with cash and opportunity.

Today you're stuck either in the same role, or perhaps you've made some strides up the corporate ladder but now your career is on pause. So, where you do start? What do you do now?

You start with the T.V. show, Scandal, first season, episode one. Yes, go to iTunes or Netflix and watch the very first episode of Scandal. No doubt you have seen the fictitious Olivia Pope on Thursday nights. I don't think there's a woman around who hasn't seen Olivia Pope dressed to the nines, carrying fierce handbags, wearing designer shoes, walking in and out of meetings saying, "It's handled." It made women, especially women in Corporate America, stand up and cheer. Think back to the first episode. I've used the opening scene in several trainings on leadership. The episode opens with the character, Harrison Wright meeting a young woman in a bar. After a few quick-witted confident remarks, he tells her he's there to offer her a job. The woman doesn't seem interested at first and then gasps out loud when Harrison says, "I work for Olivia Pope. The Olivia Pope." I want to call your attention to Harrison's description of Olivia Pope. He describes working with Olivia Pope as, "the best job you'll ever have, you'll slay dragons, change lives… because Olivia Pope is as amazing as they say. When you work for Olivia you are a gladiator in a suit!"

Why is this important? If you are truly interested in getting promoted time and time again, one of the very first things you have to do is understand your personal brand and what others say about you when you're not in the room. You have to know, without a doubt, what is being said about you in meetings, at dinner tables and even at ten o'clock at night in a dimly lit bar over martinis. The next step to your promotion is your brand. Personal branding is the process of developing a "mark" that is created around your name or your career. It's what comes to mind immediately when people think of you. Just like the golden arches represent McDonald's, you have your own golden arches. There is something that immediately comes to mind when your name is mentioned. And you get to control that image. Any great marketing expert will tell you a brand is the promise of an experience. When it comes to your professional brand, it is also the promise of an experience – an experience others will have every time they encounter you.

When you think about your next promotion, who do you know is the best of the best? Who in your company or organization defines success and leadership? Who do you admire? Now think about who they are, their values, traits and their characteristics. Write them down and study them. Start really thinking about the brand you want to have. What do you want others to say about you when you're not in the room?

What Others Say About You Matters

Let's face facts, you're probably really good at your current role. Nobody thinks about promotion unless they're good at what they do. You are good at what you do. You're smart and everybody knows it. Your next promotion, each time, begins with a good, solid personal brand. Your personal brand has to be visible for all to see. When I say all, I mean all of the people who matter. That means your peers, team members, your boss and even your boss' boss. So, let's dig deeper into this personal brand.

When your name is spoken, what's the first thing that comes to mind? Let's go back to McDonald's. I don't care who you are or where you live, McDonald's is McDonald's. Children all over the world scream with sheer delight every time they see the golden arches. That's because McDonald's has a consistent brand. Think about Michael Jordan. Michael Jordan played in his final NBA game on April 16, 2003 in Philadelphia and went to the bench during the third quarter after scoring only 13 points in the game. However, grown men to this day will tell you Michael is the greatest basketball player in the world. Air Jordan still has the brand of the greatest basketball player. Now think about the name, Donald Trump. No matter who you voted for or what side of the political aisle you sit on, when you hear the name Donald Trump, a very clear picture comes to mind.

Your brand is the exact same way. What do people think of when they hear your name? When your name is spoken in meetings, what comes to mind? Are you helpful? Flexible? Dependable? Or – are you difficult? Hard to get along with? Do people like working with you?

I'm going to be brutally honest with you, people want to work with people they like. Nobody wants to spend eight hours a day with someone they don't get along with. Nobody wants to have someone on their team, particularly in a leadership role, that the team can't stand. You must have a good personal brand in the role you are in today in order to move to the next level. And each time you move up the ladder of success, you have to start over with developing that solid personal brand.

If your brand sucks (forgive me but I have to give it to you straight), you won't get the next opportunity until you fix it. Are you a Jordan or a Trump? Both will be talked about for many years to come.

Here are some tough issues to deal with on the road to a successful personal brand. This is how you master the brand principle!

1. *Master the Art of Dependability* – In plain English, come to work on time every single day. If you haven't mastered the art

of coming to work every day, promotion is not in your immediate future. If you are on any kind of disciplinary action for violating your company's attendance policy, get it together quickly.

2. *Master the art of Imitation* – Some say imitation is the sincerest form of flattery. I think imitation is one of the easiest ways to work on your personal brand. Success leaves clues, and it's your job to follow them. Who is the most successful person you know? Who does it better than anyone you know? Who is on the fast track? Who is the face of leadership at your organization? Do what they do. Watch them and imitate their success. Watch their flaws (everyone has them) or mistakes and do the opposite. Become a student of the best.

3. *Mater the art of the Company You Keep* – Successful people attract successful people. Be very careful of the company you keep, particularly at work. When you're on the road to success, who you spend time with is important. There's a Proverb that says, "Walk with the wise and become wise; associate with fools and get in trouble." Who are you being seen with at work? Be careful not to associate professionally with those who aren't interested in going where you're going. Be very careful not to spend too much time with the people

who violate the Attitude Principle. Make it a point to spend time with people who are going where you're going. Spend time with people who are on the next level – the level you aspire to be on.

4. *Master the art of Appearance* – If you want to be promoted to the level of Director, how do they dress? How do current directors dress? Dress for the role you want tomorrow, not the one you have today. In most offices today, the attire is business casual and that's perfectly fine. How are the leaders in your organization dressed? If they are not business casual, don't do it. If male leaders are in jeans but wear a tie, men, grab your tie. If the female leaders in your organization are in jeans with high heels on, don't you dare show up everyday in athletic shoes. If the next promotional opportunity comes along and the decision is down to you and another candidate and the only thing they can point to is your negative appearance, that would be a shame.

Each time you move to the next level of promotional opportunity, you have to reestablish your brand. Each level of promotion and growth requires you to start over and make sure your brand is sharp, polished and able to stand solid at this level.

In May of 2018, comedienne Roseanne Barr made one single move that destroyed her brand and paid the ultimate price of being fired. Millions of people were excited when the Roseanne show returned to television. The show's iconic reboot had been a huge success, but with one single tweet it all came crashing down. One tweet from the show's star – the woman the show was named for, ended it all. The brand of the star was forever changed. The comeback was over. The show was initially cancelled. Roseanne was fired. Rosanne's brand was changed from comedy star to racist. The show, when it returned, was rebranded without its former star.

How To Create A Stellar Brand

- **Start Thinking of Yourself as a Brand** – Decide how you want people to see you and think of you. When you are not in the room, what do you want to be said about you? Do you want to be known as the subject matter expert? What qualities or expertise do you want associated with you? Write it down and really think about it. When you think of the best leaders, the best in your field, what characteristics do they have that you want?

- **Understand Your Values**- What things do you do better than anyone else? What comes as natural talent to you? Are you a gifted writer? Are you an expert at numbers and data? What do you do instinctively? What do people often come to you for? Write down your five greatest assets.

- **Showcase Your Talents with Projects** - Discover creative ways to let others know who you are and the value that you add. List 3 projects at work you can volunteer to help with. What industry events can you attend? Just like commercials for retail products, you are a product that needs marketing. People are watching, so give them something great to watch.

- **Market Yourself on Social Media** - Even your social media is part of your personal brand. Remember whatever you post lives forever (remember Roseanne?). Ensure your posts on social media are befitting that of the leader you want to become. Your boss or other leaders within the organization may not be your friends on Facebook, but remember we are all six degrees of separation away. I can't tell you how many times someone has come into my office and shown me an unflattering social media post by an aspiring leader. It's hard to recover from, so be careful. If you currently have posts on social media that don't reflect your brand, delete them quickly.

- **Network Often** – Networking is very important to your brand. Attend networking events, conferences, seminars and other industry gatherings. Keep business cards on hand and always remember names of important people. Networking puts your brand out front and center. It helps others remember who you are and what you can offer. Rehearse your elevator pitch so you are able to clearly communicate who you are and what you offer.

- **Evolve** – Personal brands are ever evolving. As you move through the levels of leadership, your brand must evolve, and you will find yourself reinventing yourself. Brands aren't stagnant. They need to constantly be reevaluated, tweaked and improved. This is the reason why we see new commercials for the same products. It's reinventing the brand based on the needs of the consumer. Each level up requires a brand evolution.

What will be said about you in a bar at ten o'clock at night? If you manage your personal brand you will be called a gladiator, amazing, the best of the best. It starts with your brand!

Applying the Brand Principle

- Write down three to five people who have brands that you admire. What do you admire most about their brands? In what ways can you emulate these characteristics?

- List five character traits you want others to say about you when they are describing you.

- What steps can you immediately begin to take to improve your brand (appearance, dependability, etc.)?

- Review your LinkedIn account and all of your other social media outlets. Look for ways to brand yourself for the future.

- Remove any prior social media posts that don't align with your new brand.

- List two networking events/opportunities you will participate in over the next three months.

The Visibility Principle

The power of visibility can never be underestimated.

~ Margaret Cho

Once your brand begins to take shape, you will automatically find yourself being out front more often. You may find yourself taking the lead on projects, being asked for your opinions in meetings. The visibility principle will start to happen organically, but will also require you to do some work. It will require you to take action steps to not only become more visible, but to stay visible. What you do at this next level is vital to your career growth. The first step to the visibility principle is about who you surround yourself with – who's in your inner circle. In all sincerity; at this level you will lose some people along the journey. There are some people, some "work friends", who will fall by the way side. You have to be comfortable with this change. You becoming more visible calls for you to have to take a realistic look at the company you keep. When you look at your inner circle, how successful are they? How supportive are they? Where are they going in their careers? At every promotion level, this is so important. Each time you are ready to promote to the next level, you have to evaluate your relationships. You also have to know that with each promotional opportunity, some people will not make the climb with you. A few years ago, I worked with a client, Brad, who was a supervisor for a large organization. Brad wanted to get promoted to manager and we worked together to create a stellar personal brand that showcased his talents. Once he began operating within his personal brand, he started to get noticed. He was assigned a project that was sure to get him promoted. Brad had been with the organization for about four years and had developed some really good friendships with frontline employees as well as the supervisor team. However, once special projects started coming Brad's way, people started talking. His colleagues started coming down really hard on him, saying he had become "one of them". Some even accused him of spying for the management team. I remember meeting Brad for coffee one afternoon when he told me he was struggling with some of his peers. Brad had to make a decision. Either he was going to keep moving forward with what he wanted for his future or fall back and relax in his past. Thankfully, Brad chose to continue moving forward. Brad had to develop new relationships at the level he was on and also develop relationships at the manager level. My immediate advice to Brad was to find someone on his level that was also interested in being promoted. Find a partner to help hold him accountable for his growth to the next level.

Growth and development don't automatically happen. It must be intentional. You must have a plan for growth, and you have to have people around you that help support your growth. This is where the visibility principle takes shape. You begin to be more strategic with who you spend time with. If you're looking to get promoted, you can't spend time in the cafeteria with the Negative Nellies – you know the folks who are always complaining about the company, the leadership team and the policies. You have to be seen as the person with solutions to problems, not the person who is complaining about problems. Becoming more visible means putting yourself out there, getting seen by people who matter. This looks like raising your hand for projects, finding unique ways to solve problems, offering your assistance to others. Here are four ways to quickly become more visible:

Take initiative. Is there a problem that the team is struggling with? Are there tasks on your boss' to-do list that he/she can never seem to get done? Is the department struggling with a performance metric? A great way to increase visibility is to take on a project or solve a problem within the business. What problem can you solve for your boss or the team? Take the initiative and create a plan for solving that problem. Present it to your boss or leadership team and get to work. The words, "that's not my job" should never enter your mind and certainly not your vocabulary. Your job description is a starting point, not an ending point.

Take on additional responsibility. One of the easiest ways to become more visible is by taking on more responsibility. In addition to performing your current duties well, taking on additional responsibility helps your boss and other leaders see you in a different light. This doesn't mean you should kill yourself. However, if a new project or responsibility comes along that would help you expand your skills, take advantage of it.

Under promise and over commit. This is a very simple way to become more visible. If you know it will take you three days to complete the project, commit to completing it within five days. Then deliver a great product in three days. Complete your assignments by giving more than required and doing it in less time than you committed whenever possible. Exceeding expectations is a great way to show your boss, and those around you, how great you are and how well you execute.

Show up and do your best every time. No matter how large or small the assignment, always, always give 100%. Be known for delivering a superior product with an outstanding work ethic. Never complete anything with less than your best work. By doing your best work, you are showing the leaders within your organization what you are capable of, and they will start to rely on you more and more.

Literally be visible. Spend time each day greeting your coworkers. Make a point to say good morning to everyone on the team each day. Give kudos and acknowledgement to your coworkers when they do a great job. This becomes part of your brand as a team player.

Get involved in charity work. Most organizations have charity events or volunteer opportunities throughout the year. Get involved in your organization's charity events. This helps you become more visible to those outside of your immediate department.

Keep track of your accomplishments. Document your accomplishments and all of the great things you do. It's hard for your boss and other leaders to remember everything you do. Keep a running list of every assignment, project, even compliments received from others. This gives you something to talk about when it's time for your performance review. It also helps keep your resume up to date.

Becoming more visible helps others start to see you at the next level before you actually arrive there.

Applying the Visibility Principle

- What are two ways you can take initiative? What problem can you look to solve for your team or your boss?

- Pay close attention to your promises and commitments, ensuring you exceed expectations every time.

- Become more visible within your organization. Consider volunteering for special projects or company-wide causes that get you recognized outside of your immediate department.

- Look for ways to take on additional responsibilities within the team or department.

- Keep track of your accomplishments along with compliments and accolades you receive from others throughout the year.

The Mentor Principle

A mentor is someone who allows you to see the hope inside yourself.

~ Oprah Winfrey

Once you've evaluated your inner circle and started to expand your visibility, it's time to begin including people who can help push you to the next level. This means your career board of directors. At every level, you should have mentors and advocates who will push you and also champion for your success.

Oftentimes, people go to a mentor wanting them to guide their career, hold their hand and literally give them their next promotion. That's a recruiter, not a mentor. A mentor is someone you can talk to openly about where you are and what you want. However, it's not your mentor's job to get you the next promotion. It's a mentor's role to help you see things forward, to guide you and offer advice based on his/her experience. A mentor should work with you on a few very specific goals. It shouldn't be an exhaustive list. You should go to your mentor and ask for guidance in one area. I believe you should seek out a mentor for guidance in one of three areas:

- Strategic Career Guidance

- Next Level Influence

- Networking/Introductions

Choosing a mentor is not always an easy task. It took me years to find the right mentors. It was hit or miss for a long time. Why? Because at first, I was choosing the wrong people. Then I had the wrong people choosing mentors for me. I know that sounds odd, but it's true. I first chose mentors that I was in awe of – meaning people that I was star-struck by their success. In a room with these individuals, I felt so small and unworthy that it made it impossible for them to accurately mentor me. I was so star-struck that I couldn't speak openly and honestly. Next, there were several mentoring programs that I was chosen to be apart of by various organizations. I'd write an essay and someone who knew nothing about me would select a mentor for me based on what I'd written. This was an absolute disaster. It's very difficult for someone else to select a mentor for you without actually knowing you. At my core I'm very disciplined, but I'm also very creative. I change my mind often and I'm always looking to learn something new. This can be very frustrating to a mentor. Once I had a mentor chosen for me and he tried very hard to make me a mini version of himself. He was one step ahead from me in title and we argued a lot at the beginning of the arduous year-long mentoring relationship. After a few months, I stopped being truthful in my communication with him and just silently hoped for the program to be over. Shortly after the program ended, I was interviewing for a promotional opportunity. He interviewed for the same role. At this point, I wasn't sure who was mentoring who if we were both going for the same job. No worries, though – I got the job!

What this taught me is that I have to be very selective in choosing my mentors – the people I allow to pour into my career. For many years following this experience, I allowed books to mentor me. Eventually, I moved on to YouTube and TedTalks. Today I have three very great mentoring relationships. One is with an individual I met after hearing a speech she gave on YouTube. I reached out to her and offered to pay her for two hours of her time the next time she was in town. She offered me a ticket to an upcoming conference she was hosting. I attended the conference and spent 20 minutes with her. For one year following that initial meeting, she allowed me 15 minutes of her time once a month at no charge. My other mentor is a CEO of a large corporation. He lives in another state and we talk on the phone once a month for 30 minutes on his drive home. I have not been in a room with two of my mentors for almost three years but consider these leaders to be my mentors and my great friends. My third mentor is a Vice President of a Fortune 500 company. I heard him give a speech at a function and his career journey sounded a lot like mine. I reached out through another leader within the company and he has recently become my mentor.

Now I know you're wondering why I have so many mentors. The answer is simple – each mentor pours into a different area of my career. The first mentor helps me through networking. She is a powerful writer and speaker and she has helped introduce me to some really great people in the speaking community. When I'm preparing to speak or write, she's who I turn to. The CEO helps me prepare for my next level of influence. He helps me with building my confidence as I step out of my comfort zone with training and developing leaders. This helps me tremendously, as I am now coaching leaders at an executive level. The third mentor is my mentor within the HR world. Although we have only begun working together, he helps me with executive presence within the HR realm. Do you need three mentors? Only you can decide. I will tell you that for many years, I only had one mentor. I go into each mentoring relationship asking for six months. The mentor decides if it should continue. I like to think I give as much as I take from my mentors. I'm always looking for ways to add value to them. This is the best way to learn. If my mentor is working on a project, I offer to proofread. I might offer to do small tasks like making copies for a presentation. If my mentor is speaking at an event, I will always ask to attend and lend support. I will be the one carrying his notes, water, mints or extra pens. I enjoy my time with each of my mentors, because I am able to learn little nuggets of wisdom from each of them.

What do we talk about? When you only have 15 or 30 minutes, you have to get right to the point. Mentors who are at least two levels ahead of you in title don't have time to waste. Typically, I ask each of my mentors 3-5 questions during our time together. Here is a list of questions I have asked over the years:

22 Questions to Ask Your Mentor:

1. What are your daily habits?

2. What are 3 things you do every single day?

3. Success can be defined in many ways. How do you define success?

4. What values guide your decisions?

5. What accomplishment are you most proud of?

6. What's the greatest piece of advice you've ever received?

7. What do you wish you knew at my stage of life or career?

8. What are you learning right now?

9. What are you currently reading?

10. What positive thing do you see in me that I need to focus on developing?

11. What are some obstacles that I DON'T see that might be preventing me from moving forward?

12. Who or what do you know that I should know?

13. What can I do to help you?

14. How do you spend most of your time?

15. What would you do if you were me?

16. Is where you are in your career where you thought you'd end up?

17. Was there ever a time where you felt like you were failing? What did you do?

18. Has there ever been a time in your career when you felt stuck? What did you do?

19. I had a situation that happened last week that I'm not sure I handled in the best way. Can you help me think through what to do differently next time?

20. What skills do you use most in your current position?

21. What advice would you like to have heard when you were first starting out?

22. If you had to teach me something you've learned over the last 30 days, what would it be?

They key thing I've learned about seeking out a mentor is that a great mentor doesn't have to be someone you have a lot in common with. A great mentor doesn't necessarily even have to be on the same career path. A great mentor is someone who is at least two levels ahead of you in title and someone who listens to your perspective, your unique way of thinking. The mentor then comes along side you and helps broaden both your perspective and your way of thinking. The best mentor is someone who knows the way, goes the way and then graciously shows you the way.

Applying the Mentor Principle

- Look for someone to become your mentor. Seek out a successful leader who is at least two titles ahead of you and ask them to have coffee with you or a quick phone call. During this discussion, ask them questions about their career and tell them the direction you are looking to go in your career. Ask for one piece of advice. This will help you see if this is someone who could possibly be a good mentor for you.

- Once you secure a mentor, be proactive in the relationship. Schedule calls or meetings once a month and come prepared with the things you wish to discuss.

- During each mentoring discussion, have prepared the things you previously discussed, the action you have taken based on the advice of the mentor and one or two questions to ask them at each session.

- Be sure to find ways to add value to your mentor. Look for ways to help lighten your mentor's load.

- Always say thank you to your mentor. Following each mentoring session, send a note or an email thanking your mentor for their time.

Influence Principle

"Leadership is influence...nothing more, nothing less."

~ John C. Maxwell

Our success at work often lies in our ability to influence those around us. With every promotion comes a greater opportunity to influence. With greater influence comes greater responsibility. You may not start out as someone who leads a team, but with each level of promotion, your leadership grows, and your level of influence expands. At the writing of this book, I have not managed a team greater than five, meaning I've never had more than five people who report directly to me. However, my level of influence as an executive coach, leadership trainer and human resource professional expands to reach upwards of five hundred people every day. It doesn't matter how many people report to you, what matters is how many people you have the ability to reach and ultimately influence. Many times, we think promotion is about making sure the spotlight is on us. Quite the contrary – it's about being the one holding the spotlight. If you're the one holding the spotlight on others, those people become a microphone –

screaming to everyone who will listen how great you are. In order to become a person of influence, you have to take the focus off of yourself and put it squarely on others. Influence is what makes people want to work with you. It's what makes people want to follow your lead. Here's how you gain influence:

Integrity – Everyone thinks they have integrity, but what you think doesn't matter. Do others believe you have integrity? Does your team think you have integrity? Do the leaders in the position to promote you believe you are a person with integrity? Integrity is your ability to do the right thing for others and the organization as a whole. Can others come to you for good advice knowing that you will guide them in the right direction?

Trust – Can others trust you? Your next promotion is about trust. If you are the person in the cafeteria or break room gossiping about your coworkers or your leaders, you are not trustworthy. Do you keep your word? Do you show up and do what you say you're going to do? Can your leaders trust you to do what you say? If no one is watching, can you be trusted? With every new promotion comes a new level of trust.

People – Influence is all about your ability to take care of people. Yes, you want to be promoted, but you can't do anything without people. How are you taking care of the people on the team? Who are you helping to become better? Influence is about your ability to attract others to what you're doing. People want to learn from, growth with and follow greatness. Leadership is not always about who has the highest title in the room. True leadership is about the person who has the most influence in the room. In meetings, watch the room to see who has the most influence. Also watch who gives the most resistance, or the most push-back when new ideas surface. People want to follow people who are going places. Be very careful who and what you follow. Be the kind of person who is seeking to gain good, positive influence.

Presence – Professional presence is about how you show up – how you show up in meetings with your boss and throughout the entire organization. Your presence is the energy you bring to every meeting whether it's a meeting with your peers or even a brief encounter in the cafeteria. Is your presence bringing positivity and optimism, or does it bring frustration and negativity? Learn to carry yourself for the position you want in five years. When you enter a room, enter it as if you are the leader you aspire to be.

Your next promotion is closely tied to your level of influence at all levels. Influence is about your ability to motivate and inspire others to take action in a positive way. The best leaders are those who can successfully influence up, down and across the organization. Creating positive influence will not only be a catalyst to your own success, it will become the legacy you will leave behind. The principles of influence will also include your ability to:

- Lead and Work with Integrity
- Have Credibility with People
- Have Faith in People
- Effectively Listen to People
- Understand People
- Grow and Develop People
- Navigate for People
- Connect with People
- Learn from People
- Empower People

Notice how these steps have less to do with you and more to do with others. Leadership is about other people. Without other people there is no leader. Leadership is influence – nothing more, nothing less. Learn to act with integrity, trust and professional presence. When you do, people will follow you anywhere.

Applying the Influence Principle

- In what ways are you ensuring you come across to leaders and team members as being credible and trustworthy? Spend time watching how others respond to you in meetings, ensuring you are gaining positive influence.

- Make an sincere effort to listen to other people, to value their thoughts and opinions.

- Within your organization, list the names of those with the most influence. What character traits and leadership abilities do they display?

- Are you growing in a way that draws people to you? As you grow and learn new things, be sure to share your knowledge and expertise with others.

- Ask a trusted friend or even your boss for feedback on your professional presence. Ask them to rate your tone, attitude and appearance in meetings.

Strength Principle

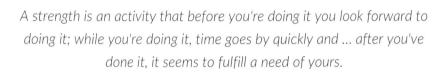

A strength is an activity that before you're doing it you look forward to doing it; while you're doing it, time goes by quickly and ... after you've done it, it seems to fulfill a need of yours.

~ Marcus Buckingham

Most companies hire employees based on the things they say they can do well. However, once hired, the company uses every performance review conversation to highlight the areas of weakness. If you want to learn one of the most important principles of promotion, learn to play to your strengths. As you grow in leadership, make sure your team members are also playing to their strengths.

Successful leaders know the importance of consistently playing to their strengths. Never waste time focusing on the areas you're not naturally gifted at – and by all means, don't try to be a jack of all trades. Years ago, I was doing everything I could to get promoted. I spoke with the Vice President of my department and asked her what it would take for me to get promoted. She told me that most people at that next level were very gifted analytically. If I wanted to be promoted, I would have to become much more analytical. She told me the future roles within our department would call for me to do what analysts do. I spent the next six months trying to become a master at excel spreadsheets and all things data. I ran reports, tried to analyze data and I basically made myself sick. To say I am not naturally gifted at numbers and data would be an understatement. In fact, it would be down right laughable. I spent six months trying to be something I was not. Finally, after a meeting where I was called upon to read out from some data that I'm pretty sure I had gotten wrong, another leader took me aside and said the magic words. "Andrea, you suck at numbers. You will never get promoted that way." I was shocked, offended and my feelings were deeply hurt. This great leader looked me square in the eyes and went on to tell me that I needed to play to my strengths. I would never get promoted trying to do something I wasn't good at. Yes, I could become better, but I would never outshine someone who was naturally gifted at analytics. I went on a crusade to discover my strengths. This led me to a wonderful book that was then called *Now Discover Your Strengths*. It has since been revised and called *Strength Finders 2.0*. The authors of the book and the company that founded the research believe that each person has their own unique strengths. They have discovered that everyone operates from four distinct domains of strength: **Executing, Influencing, Relationships**

Building and Strategic Thinking. According to their latest research, there are 34 strengths that fall into these four areas, and we are all only good at a few things. According to *Strength Finders 2.0,* we all have five key strengths. As this translates to our careers and our promotional opportunities, I believe most of these strengths blend together, so we are only really good at two to five different things. Once you discover your strengths, do what you can to spend most of your time playing to them. Don't worry about your weaknesses. Statistics show you will never get significantly better at your weaknesses. Even if you spent two hours a day working your weaknesses, you might only get one to two percent better at them over the course of one year. However, if you spent one hour a day working on your areas of strength, over the course of one year you would improve these qualities by thirty to forty percent. If you work on your weaknesses, you will never excel. The best you could be is average, and nobody will pay for average. Companies only pay and promote the best. Spend your time working on your strengths. This what I call bankrolling your brilliance. Here's how to bankroll your brilliance:

Discover what your strengths are. This could look like simply paying attention to your emotions while you work. What tasks or assignment energize you? What areas are you naturally gifted in? What assignments can you do so well that you lose track of time? These are your strength areas. Also consider purchasing the *Strength Finders* book and taking their online assessment. It will be the best twenty dollars you could ever spend on your career.

Trade your strengths for your weaknesses. This is where you begin to form partnerships and alliances with people who are gifted in areas where you are weak. This looks like partnering with others in areas where you are not strong. I am lousy at running reports and all things excel, and I've discovered that most people who are naturally gifted with numbers and reports are not typically comfortable communicating publically. In every role I've had since discovering my strengths, I have partnered with someone else to help run numbers for me in exchange for me giving presentations and speeches for them. Even in my business, I have formed really strategic partnerships with other entrepreneurs where I write for them in exchange for their gift of numbers, reporting and financial advice.

Look for assignments that showcase your strengths. Once you know your strengths and are operating in them most of the time, look for assignments that showcase your talents. If you discover a strength area in execution, meaning your strength is in getting things done with speed, accuracy and precision, find ways to showcase this to others who matter.

Communicate your strengths to others. You are probably one of the best kept secrets in your organization. It's time to let the secret out. Sit down with your boss and help him/her understand your strengths. Put a plan in place to have a conversation about your future goals and aspirations, utilizing your signature strengths. Ask for special projects and assignments in this area and when you are given the opportunity, over deliver. Do more than is required and let your leaders know how much you enjoyed it.

The Strength Principle is designed to help you follow a simple leadership pattern called the 70-25-5 Giving Rule:

- Give 70 percent of your time to your areas of strength.
- Give 25 percent of your time to the areas you want to improve.
- Give 5 percent of your time to the areas of your weakness.

I would be remiss if I didn't address your areas of weakness. As I mentioned, I am terrible at reports and financial matters (other than counting money). There are times when you can't delegate or trade your strengths for your weakness. While it's true that focusing on your strength and leveraging others to help with your weak areas will lead you to more success, there are about five percent of things you have to do and may not always have other around to partner with you. I make myself run monthly reports in my business just to make sure I can do it. I sit with friends and business partners and even my team members who are great at running excel spreadsheets and dig into data once a month for thirty minutes. I watch them run my reports and I ask them to teach me something. I write down what I've learned in a notebook and I teach back what I've learned.

There will always be things about your role that you just simply do not like or are not good at. When you put the Strength Principle into place, you will only have to spend about 5% of the time on these things, so get them done quickly and move on to your strengths.

Applying the Strength Principle

- When you are "in the zone", the times when you're working and you lose track of time, what are you doing?

- Consider purchasing a copy of *Strength Finders 2.0* to uncover your five key areas of strength.

- Once you discover your strengths, begin working on developing one or two key strengths. This could look like taking a class or seminar or reading a book to grow your strengths.

- Look for ways to work more in your areas of strength in your current role.

- Share your areas of strength with your boss, asking for ideas on ways to play to them in your role.

Communication Principle

The art of communication is the language of leadership.

~ James Humes

Being able to effectively communicate at all levels within an organization is a skill that everyone needs to master. Yet, most of my clients struggle in this area. In the world of text messages and social media, our business communication skills leave a lot to be desired. It is imperative in a leadership role that you communicate effectively, and communication is a skill that we should always work on. The greater your level of influence, the more important good communication skills become. The communication principle encourages you to improve on how you communicate with others. This principle is about sharpening your communication skills.

The key to mastering the communication principle is to remember that your communication is not about you. It's always about the other person. Your job is to communicate in a way that the other person not only hears, but after listening is encouraged to move forward in a positive and productive manner. Presidential speech writer James

Humes says it best, "The art of communication is the language of leadership." Learn to speak the language. Speak it often and speak it well. I love the thought of communication being an art form. When you think of an artist, you think of someone who is focused on bringing something they've created to life. An artist is able to create something meaningful and then share it with the world in a way that makes the world not only see it, but also feel it. Think about musicians and singers. A musician creates a piece of music, or a song, and sings it in a way that draws the audience in and makes them feel deep emotions. That's what effective communication does. It's an art form. It's what you use to create, to draw others into your world and then make them feel. When you're communicating, you are attempting to get your message across to someone else. Like an artist, you start with a blank canvas and as you begin to speak, you draw a picture for others to see. There are many tools we use to become masters of communication. When it comes to the communication principle relative to getting promoted, we communicate by writing, speaking and even with our non-verbal emotions. How you communicate in writing is just as important as how you communicate verbally. Use professional language when you're writing, whether you are writing an email or even a text message. If it's business, write it using business language. No one ever has to guess what you mean if you write it using proper grammar. Also, use words that everyone understands. No one wants to have to use a dictionary to decipher an email or a memo. Your business communication must. Next, is your ability to speak. More specifically, this is about the words you select. People judge you by the words you use – words have power. The words you choose matter, particularly in the business world. Remember, your words are creating a picture for the listener. Use words that are positive, powerful and concise. Avoid using words that contradict the direction you want to go in. Slang is one example, foul language is another. Use words that will take you forward in your career. Many people watch their hard work go up in smoke because they spoke harshly or used bad language in a meeting.

I want to share with you my playbook for communicating effectively:

Master the art of conversation – In other words, watch what you say and how you say it. Become an expert communicator. Leaders rise and fall by their communication style. Great leaders are very careful with their words, because they understand the power of what they say. Foul language is the death of many careers.

Get good at presentation – I feel some of you cringing right now, but it's really not necessary. In order to move through the levels of leadership, you have to be able to present – something! You may not be comfortable giving ninety-minute speeches. However, you have to be able to present clear, concise ideas. You have to be able to present in front of, at the very least, a few people. The higher up you go in any organization, the more you will have to present, so start practicing now.

Get to the point quickly. In her book *Shut Up And Say Something,* Communications Coach, Karen Friedman gives the best advice I can think of when she talks about getting to the point in a quick and concise manner. In business, time is money. Don't waste your time or the time of others with too many words. Whether this is in email, voicemail or in person, keep it short, simple and to the point.

Watch your words. Simply put, not everyone is on the same page when it comes to vocabulary. In order to be effective in your communication, use words that are easily understood. Do not use words that someone has to pull out a dictionary to find their meaning. Also, never use slang or swear words when communicating in business. I know this seems silly to write, but you'd be surprised at how many emails I've seen using colorful language.

Know your audience. You communicate with your friends much differently than you communicate with your boss. It's important to understand who you're communicating with and what they need from you. In business, we have to adjust our communication style to our audience. You have to understand how the other party wants to give and receive information. One of my favorite leaders is the most articulate man I know. When he speaks, everyone stops what they are doing, and they listen. However, when he wants information from others, he wants it quick and to the point. He doesn't want to listen for hours on end; he wants to hear what you have to say and get back to his day. Another leader may want every single detail, she may want to hear every strategy you tried and how you came up with this magic number. If that's what she wants, give it to her. Learning your audience takes time and attention to detail.

Plan out your talk track. This is the number one strategy in my playbook. Every important conversation is written down and well thought out. Never wing the important conversations. If you have an idea for how to improve performance, write down your conversation to your team and plan out what you want to say. I recommend to my clients that for each important conversation, they draft up a paragraph or two for exactly how they want the conversation to flow. This is not necessarily a script, but it serves as an exercise to hear how the conversation will go. I encourage clients to think through all of the things the other person could say and think about a response for every option.

Watch your tone. This is true in written and spoken communication. Your tone can kill a message, even one that is meant to be positive and encouraging. Research shows that only 7% of meaning comes from the words you speak, while 38% comes from your tone of voice and speech patterns. This means people are listening to your tone much more than they are hearing your word choice. When speaking, pay close attention to your tone and also how the other person is responding.

Be professional, polite and gracious. Any instance of communication can be improved by adding "please" and "thank you". Grow your communication skills by being gracious with your words. This will become one of your greatest assets as you move up the corporate ladder. Being courteous, respectful and polite goes a lot further than you could imagine.

If you can't say it nicely, don't say it. I think every mother taught us this lesson, and it's true even in business. If you can't say something nice about someone, don't say anything. Gossip and slander are a dangerous trap that should be avoided at all cost.

Consider joining a professional speaking organization. Speaking and communicating is vitally important as you grow in any leadership role. You may want to consider joining a speaking organization like

ToastMasters or the National Speakers Association to help you improve your public speaking and communication skills.

Applying the Communication Principle

- Begin paying close attention to the way you communicate in meetings, over the phone and in email. Identify areas for improvement.

- Consider joining a speaking organization to improve your speaking and presentation skills i.e. Toastmasters or National Speakers Association.

- Look for opportunities to speak or present before an audience (your peers, your boss, etc.)

- Before speaking, be sure to plan out your speech. Whether you're speaking in a meeting, giving a presentation or providing feedback, write out your conversation and practice it.

Growth Principle

Without continual growth and progress, such words as improvement, achievement, and success have no meaning.

~ Benjamin Franklin

Many leaders struggle because they stop learning, and ultimately stop growing. Let's face it, anything you don't feed will eventually die. The same holds true for your career and your own development. The best leaders are always learning, growing and trying new things. Look at Oprah, Magic Johnson and Richard Branson. These individuals could all have taken their one-time success and called it quits. They each had enough money years ago to retire on an island and sip tropical drinks while their money earned more money. Instead, they all knew the importance of continuous growth. Every year, somewhere around September, I begin looking back at the previous nine months and make a growth plan for the new year. I take a careful look at the things I enjoyed, the things I accomplished; and I also look at the things I absolutely hated, the things that drained me. During this Fall season, I put together a plan for growth that will help push me forward. I'm super serious about my own growth, the growth of my leaders and the growth of the clients I coach. When I hear someone say they are struggling to get promoted, I've learned to ask two questions. The first one is: What have you done in the last twelve months to develop yourself? The second question is: What have you done in the last twelve months to help develop others?

Growth doesn't just happen. It is possible to be in the same position for ten years and not know anything more than you did ten years ago. Growth has to be intentional. Writing this book was part of my intentional growth and the intentional growth of my clients. As we discussed in the Strength Principle, we are all only really good at about two to five things. Every year, we should focus on how to get better at two to three of those things.

I have a fun fascination with GPS systems and Apps that help give directions. One of the reasons is because I'm always lost. I have no sense of direction. I'm the girl who needs landmarks for directions. If you tell me there's a gas station on one corner and a McDonald's on the other, I'll find it. If you tell me to go south four blocks and then head east, I will never arrive at the destination. One of my favorite apps is Waze – which I believe is the best app on the planet. This precious gem can lead you around traffic and construction and is updated in real-time by its users as they drive. It even alerts you to when the police are nearby.

The Growth Principle is like an app that helps you get to your destination. Your growth as you look towards your next promotion should not be about a title. It should be about your overall leadership. Leadership is not determined by how many positions you climb within your organization. It's not about how many promotions you obtain. To be quite candid, the higher up you go within any corporation, the less promotional opportunities there are. Think about it, how many Vice Presidents are there at your company? How many Presidents? CEOs? The Growth Principle is all about growing and developing yourself to ensure you stay relevant. You are in charge of developing your career and your leadership skills. As you grow in your career, the less development you will receive from your boss. At the manager level, often times there are no assigned classes for you to take, and there's no curriculum to help with moving up. There are also no CEO classes. It is your responsibility alone, and it is a responsibility not to be taken lightly. When it comes to getting promoted, intentional growth is a sure-fire way to ensure your next promotion. Imagine what next year could look like if you seriously activated the Growth Principle. Who would you be in twelve months if you intentionally put together a plan, a navigation system, to help you arrive at a pre-planned destination?

The growth principle starts with identifying, first and foremost, your destination. In twelve months, where would you like to be? Would you like to be promoted to supervisor, to manager, to Vice President? Even if you don't know the exact tittle, you have to know one thing, that you'd like to be better than you are today. Next, identify two areas you want to intentionally grow in. Listed below are six areas of professional growth with a brief definition.

1. **Communication** – Communicating effectively as a leader (written and oral communication).

2. **Execution Excellence** – Consistently completing tasks and assignments by setting realistic plans and objectives.

3. **Strategic Thinking** – Ability to envision and strategize future business objectives.

4. **Teamwork** – Collaborating and working effectively with a team.

5. **Leadership** – Ability to lead yourself and others, while consistently developing leadership skills.

6. **Relationships** – Developing business relationships both inside and outside of the organization that align with current and future goals.

Applying the Growth Principle

- Invest one hour each day in your growth areas.

- Read an article on professional or personal growth every Monday morning.

- Listen to 15-20 minutes of a leadership book on your morning or evening drive. Audible.com has a great selection of leadership books. If you listened to a leadership book for 15 minutes every work day, you will have read at least 10 books by the end of the year.

- Follow growth professionals on social media. A few of my favorites include, John Maxwell, Sheryl Sandberg, Erika Andersen, Brendon Burchard, Paul Martinelli, John Mattone, Marcia Reynolds and Grant Cardone. You'd be surprised at what you learn from a growth professional's feed on social media.

- Take a class or attend a seminar to help grow your areas of strength.

- Join an association that is directly tied to your organization or area of expertise and serve on a committee.

- Stay up to date on your industry by reading trade newsletters, articles or books that help keep you up-to-date on trends and technology. If your company has a website, make a point to read what's going on within the organization every week.

The Habits Principle

"We are, what we repeatedly do. Excellence then is not an act, but a habit."

~ Aristotle

A ndrea, why are you always here so early?" This is a question I get asked at least three times a year. My answer is always the same, "It's a habit." I'm early for everything. I hate to be late and it makes me crazy when others are late. I've made habit of being early; it gives me time to prepare. I'm early for interviews, appointments with clients, work, everything. As you recall, years ago I had a habit of being late. Now, I understand the importance of being on time. Now, I like to get in early and get prepared before the day starts. I like to calm my nerves before a speech or presentation. It's my habit because it works for me. Successful people have habits, things they do on a regular basis that contributes to their success.

Just ask Kevin Kruse. He's a New York Times bestselling author who interviewed over 200 successful people to discover their habits. One of the things he learned is that they all follow daily or monthly habits –

things they do on a consistent basis. When it comes to your career, habits are important. It ensures you remain consistent on your path to promotion. What habits do you need to begin? What habits do you need to break? It all starts with four habits to break, and then I'll give you five habits to consider:

Break These Habits:

The **"It's not my job"** habit – Break the habit of only doing what's required and feeling like it's not your job to do certain things. Get into the habit of doing what needs to be done.

The **being late and leaving early habit** – A former boss used to say, "To be on time is to be late." Starting work at 8:00 and punching out exactly at 5:00 is for workers, people with jobs. It's not for leaders and people who have careers they love. I've made a habit of arriving to work before everyone else. It gives me time to think and relax before everyone else arrives. What I've learned is the most successful executives also do this as well. They either arrive early, or they stay late after everyone else has gone. There's something very relaxing about being in the office when very few people are there. It can be the most productive time of the day.

The griping, gossiping and complaining habit – Complaining solves nothing, and nobody wants to hear it except for the people who have made a career out of complaining and griping. Successful people find solutions instead of complaining. Gossiping is probably the worst habit you can have. Every organization has problems, but you should not be the person to pontificate these problems in the cafeteria or in the parking lot. When gossip is happening, walk far away and walk quickly.

The being unprepared or unfocused habit – Just like being late, being unprepared is a bad habit. If you're attending a meeting, spend a few minutes reading over the agenda. If you're attending your weekly meeting with your boss, prepare your talking points. At the bare minimum, bring a pen and paper to meetings and be prepared to listen. One of my favorite leaders before every team meeting instruct her team, "Be where your feet are." This means, be present and attentive to what's going on where you are. Don't waste time thinking about other things when your focus should be in the now. Your lack of focus and preparation is disrespectful to the leader and inconsiderate to others.

Now let's get to the new habits. I've always been really fascinated by high achievers, successful people in their chosen field. In recent years, I've really studied the best athletes, performers and business people.

I've learned that they are fiercely disciplined with certain habits. What do the most successful people out there—the ones who get promotions, raises, and opportunities seemingly handed to them—do that everyone else doesn't? They have habits in place that help them get seen, get heard and, ultimately, get promoted.

Incorporate these habits:

- **Plan your day in advance** – Let's face it, everybody can't be early every day. That's my habit, but it may not work for your life. Perhaps you're the one who drives the kids to school every morning and getting to work at the crack of dawn doesn't work for you. You can, however, plan your day in a way that allows you to hit the ground running when you arrive. This could look like getting up thirty minutes earlier and reviewing your calendar or to-do-list. You might spend thirty minutes before bed planning out your day.

- **Have something to say** – Remember, this is about getting promoted. Your words are important. In meetings, speak up and always say something important. This isn't about using a lot of words or showing off, it's about ensuring your voice is heard as a leader. In meetings, watch for opportunities to express your opinions. People who want to get ahead don't wait for permission or an invitation to speak – they find ways to contribute. If you have a suggestion, speak up. Speak up to advocate for a peer. If someone looks unclear, ask questions on their behalf.

- **Spend quality time with your boss** – Most people have regular one-on-one meetings with their boss. If you do not, request thirty minutes once a month with your direct boss. Use this time to ask questions and ask for feedback. Your boss should know your plans for promotion. There's no greater compliment to a good leader than to help someone else succeed. Share your plans with your boss and set up regular time to connect.

- **Get to know the leaders within your organization** – If your goal is to be a manager, get to know the managers. Stop by in the morning (hint, hint) and say hello, ask how their day is going. If your Vice President is visiting the office on Tuesday, make a point to stop by and say hello. Ask him or her a quick question. Always remind them of your name and what you do.

- **Know your bar speech** – Ten years ago, after a particularly bad day, I met some friends for a drink in a nearby steak house. I arrived early and stopped at the bar for a well-deserved dirty martini. I had forgotten to take off my work identification card and a man at the bar noticed. He asked how I liked working for the company. The "politician" in me gave him my speech about how I had the pleasure of working as a human resources manager for the best company on the planet. He smiled and went on about his way. The next day, I was called into a meeting the meet the new Senior Vice President of the Division. It was the gentleman from the night before. If you find yourself in a bar with an executive from your organization, do you know what to say? Craft your bar speech and never deviate from it. Whether you're in a bar or in an elevator, you should be able to clearly articulate what you do and your career plans in less than sixty seconds.

- **Touch it once** – How may times have you opened a piece of mail and put it back on the table to do something with it later? How many times have you read an email and marked it "unread" again so you could come back to it later? Make a habit of touching it once. If it takes less than ten minutes to complete it, get it done the first time you touch it. It reduces stress and saves you time. It won't be the thing sitting in the back of your mind that you need to do.

- **Journal** – We've covered the importance of learning and reading. Most leaders have also learned the importance of journaling or writing every day. Most people think journaling is used to record their daily tasks or to vent problems; but when it comes to your career, journaling is used to chronicle your plan, your dreams. Journaling empowers you to take your raw ideas and turn them into reality. There's a Proverb that says what you write becomes reality. What's written is real. Once the words hit the paper, the image hits the imagination. Journaling, when done consistently, helps you plan out the vision and direction for your life and your career. In an interview on continuous success, Greek shipping magnate, Aristotle Onassis once said, "Carry a notebook. Write everything down... that's the million-dollar lesson they don't teach you in business school."

Applying the Habits Principle

- Make a list of habits you need to break and make a decision to break any bad habits you may have.

- Decide to incorporate two new habits that will help you become a better leader.

- Plan out your day either first thing in the morning or the night before.

- Make a list of the leaders in your organization. Review their LinkedIn pages or their company bios.

- Create your "bar speech" or "elevator pitch" in case you find yourself face-to-face with an executive within the company. This speech is what you say about your work and your company without fail.

The Executive Presence Principle

Every day you are on an interview. Dress like it, talk like it, behave like it." This is a statement I once heard a CEO make to a room filled to capacity with leaders. When I first heard this statement, I didn't understand it. The room was filled with leaders from the manager level all the way up through the CFO. Why would the CEO make this statement? Today, I clearly understand. Long before you enter a room to interview or discuss your next promotional opportunity, you have been on an interview every day leading up to that day. If you are looking to get promoted within your organization, you should know that you have been strategically watched for how you will perform at the next level. You have been interviewing every day. This speaks specifically to what is known as executive presence. Each time you reach for the next level of promotion, you will also need to establish that next level of executive presence. So, what is executive presence? Executive presence is the intersection, the moment where communication, connection, composure, credibility and humility meet. It's your ability to inspire, engage, align and move people to act. It's who shows up most often in meetings, in conversations and it's who you are when you're not there. Executive presence is your invitation and permanent seat at the table on the next level.

Executive presence ties directly to your brand. Long after you leave a room, people are still engaged with your executive presence, or lack thereof.

Why is it so important to have executive presence at every promotional level? Your executive presence, again, is your seat at the table. Executive presence is how you show up consistently and it determines whether you will gain access to opportunities. This goes back to your professional brand – but at the next level. Know this: all important decisions about you will be made when you're not in the room. Every career decision, whether it's discussions about highly visible projects, critical assignments or promotions, happen when you're not in the room; it is solely based on your presence – what you've shown of yourself consistently. Executive presence helps you gain access to those conversations. It's your ability to influence others and to represent the team, the department, the company and the organization at large.

Think about having to send a representative to speak on behalf of your company at an important event. Would you have the executive presence to be in a room filled with leaders on your level and also leaders above your current level? Would you be able to have an executive level of presence in a room filled with CEOs, Vice Presidents, Directors, Managers and Supervisors? Would your boss be comfortable having you sit in a room with other leaders? Executive presence determines what rooms you will have access to, and it's based on predictable behaviors that you have shown in the past. Executive presence has six key components:

1. **Self Awareness** – Knowing clearly who you are and what your strengths, gifts and talents are

2. **Communication** – Your ability to speak, write and interact with others at all levels

3. **Connection** – Your skill to connect professionally with others in a way that gains influence and buy-in

4. **Composure** – Self-control in every situation

5. **Credibility** – What you say and do is believable and can be counted on

6. **Humility** – Your ability to receive feedback and respond in a coachable, flexible way

Let's look closely at each of the six components.

Self-awareness – Self-awareness is about knowing who you are and the value you add. It's about knowing your strengths, gifts and talents. It's also about knowing your blind spots. Blind spots are skill gaps, behavioral issues, or areas of personal vulnerability that can hinder your growth. Self-awareness helps you stay in your lane, so to speak. It helps you not sign up for projects that don't speak to your areas of greatness. It prevents you from chasing money and titles and helps you stay focused. When you have self-awareness, you have a vision for your career and anything that does not line up with your vision, you will not participate in. Self-awareness is also about your individual mindset. It's about knowing your value, knowing exactly what you bring to the table in every situation and staying firm in that place.

Communication – How you communicate in every situation is vitally important to your success. Communication is how you speak, write and interact with others. Most people speak without thinking. In today's society we see social media posts that are written in anger or in moments of heated emotion. Oftentimes, people forget who they are and what is expected of them, and they say things that diminish their reputation and their professional brand. Learn to communicate in a way that speaks to the reputation you want to have. Plan your communication – never speak without thinking and by all means, do not write emails, memos or even social media posts without asking yourself if it speaks to the brand you have established. One email written in anger or one emotional outburst in a meeting can tank your career for years.

Connection – Developing the skill of connecting professionally with people can catapult your career forward. Connecting professionally gives you a voice of influence in every room, especially rooms you are not in. When you learn to connect professionally with people at all levels, you gain influence at all levels. Connection speaks to your ability to bring people together and move an agenda forward.

Composure – How many times have you seen leaders lose it in meetings? We've all seen leaders lose their tempers or completely fall apart when things don't go their way. Composure is about self-control. It's about controlling your emotions and staying in a position of power during tough situations. Composure is about how you respond when good things happen and also when things don't go as planned. If someone else loses control, how do you respond? When the pressure is on and work becomes crazy, how do you respond? When you're under pressure to meet a deadline and at the last minute things change, how composed are you? Learning to lead yourself is the most important step to leadership.

Credibility – How credible are you? Credibility is your ability to do what you committed to doing and doing it well. It's the level of trust others place in you. Credible leaders are honest and trustworthy. They have no hidden agendas and they want everyone to win. When you are credible, you have the trust of everyone involved. You have a proven track record of success and others are quick to follow your lead because they know they can trust you.

Humility – Author Rick Warren once said, "True humility is not thinking less of yourself; it is thinking of yourself *less.*" When you learn the component of humility, you are selfless and much more concerned about the outcome than you are about yourself. Humility is about your ability to bounce back from failures and letdowns. It's also about your ability to receive feedback, help and direction. Humility is determined by your ability to have success and not become ego-driven. Even when you win, humility helps you understand you didn't get there on your own and that you need to keep growing, learning and helping others in order to continue to be successful. Humility is inclusive, not exclusive.

Learning to master the principle of executive presence is needed at every level. How you show up and present yourself to others is the key to executive presence. It will take you up the ladder of success and keep you there. You may get promoted, but if you don't learn to master executive presence at the next level you may fall right back down the ladder.

Applying the Executive Presence Principle

- Pay close attention to how you show up in meetings, be self-aware of your body language, facial expressions and the things you say.

- Prepare in advance for every meeting knowing you are an asset and add value to the conversation. Be prepared to add value based on the meeting agenda.

- Have something to say but make sure it's the right thing. Consider your ultimate objective and choose your words carefully. Speak carefully and thoughtfully, not saying more than is necessary but ensuring your words are impactful and add value in every situation.

- Strategically connect with others at all levels. Ask questions, read their verbal and non-verbal cues. Listen for clear understanding and become a champion of others.

- Remain open to feedback that helps you grow, even when it's not what you want to hear. When receiving feedback from other leaders (your peers, your boss or other leaders), listen carefully before responding. Practice a first response of, "Thank you for the feedback. I will definitely consider what you've shared with me."

- Dress the part. Wear clothes that make you feel good and also make you look good. Wear clothes that make you feel proud and powerful when you enter the room.

- Know your value. Knowing who you are and what unique value you add helps you remember to stay in your lane. Before taking on assignments or projects, ask yourself, "Does this stretch me in my area of strength?"

- Understand how others experience you. This is especially important as you move to more senior levels. Ask your boss, peers, mentor or others that you trust in leadership roles how others perceive you. Make sure to ask people who see you in a variety of situations.

- Find someone to hold you accountable for how you show up in meetings. After every meeting or interaction, ask your accountability partner for feedback.

- Build your written communication skills. Good leaders know the importance of communicating well in all areas, including their written communication skills. Before sending emails, memos, etc., make sure you have clearly articulated the message and that it is written professionally and will be clearly understood by everyone who reads it.

- Cultivate a strong network and build your "political" savvy. Organizational politics can be a good thing. They can help you navigate through the complex situations and help you build relationships at upper levels before you reach that level. People with strong executive presence learn to cultivate a network of relationships at every level, gaining positive influence with those above and below them.

- Maintain composure when stressful situations arise. How you behave when the stakes are high or when things go wrong is vitally important to your executive presence. Do you lose your temper? Do you lose patience? Are you temperamental? Those with good executive presence present themselves as calm, even-keeled, composed and in control at all times. This allows others to look to you knowing that you will effectively lead them forward.

Persistence Principle

"The only thing that I see that is distinctly different about me is I am not afraid to die on a treadmill...If we get on the treadmill together, there's two things. You're getting off first or I'm going to die... You're not going to outwork me!"

~ Will Smith

The above quote is from actor Will Smith. This quote is taken from an interview he did years ago during which he was asked about his success. He explained to the interviewer that he wasn't the smartest or the most talented, the difference was his work ethic and his persistence to his craft.

As I was writing this book, I read the book *Think and Grow Rich* with my mentor. My mentor challenged me to read the same chapter every day for fourteen days without missing a day. If I missed a day of reading the chapter, I had to start the fourteen-day clock over again. I was determined to complete the challenge without having to start over again. The chapter was on persistence.

Persistence: The firm or obstinate continuance in a course of action in spite of difficulty or opposition.

I have to admit, I have struggled with persistence in the past. Because I enjoy the process of creation so much, I get bored very quickly. Because I love to create new approaches to things, I am quick to start something new. It's part of the creative process. Yet promotion takes persistence. Repeated promotion takes an even greater level of persistence. You must learn to stay the course until it is completed. Make a decision that you will not give up on yourself. Over the last seven years, I have learned a few hard lessons in persistence. If I'm being truly candid, I think that I may have missed out on more than a few great opportunities because I gave up or changed directions too quickly. I've also watched others struggle with this principle. A great example of this happened with two of my colleagues who were seeking a promotion. Both were extremely qualified, what we would call "highly effective" in their yearly performance ratings. Both, while at the director level, had a goal of being a vice president. There was only one level between them and the vice president level – the senior director role. One colleague said she would give the company two years to promote her to senior director and another two years to promote to vice president. If it didn't happen in two years, she would leave the organization. Now, I have to give a serious side bar to this principle. Please understand that in most organizations, the higher up you go in title, the less opportunities there are available. Let's face it, there are hundreds and sometimes even thousands of entry level positions available in most organizations, but very few vice presidents. The one colleague was giving herself four years to become a vice president, basically hoping either the company grew to have a need for a new vice president role to be created, someone would leave the organization, someone would get fired or someone would die. Pretty slim odds. The other colleague had no timeline, but a very strong desire to get promoted. He worked hard and could be counted on to do more than his required share of the work – and always with a great attitude. Eventually, after about twelve months and a restructuring of one department, a new senior director position was created. They both applied for the role. Neither got the position. The one colleague was devastated, and it showed. She told everyone who would listen how hard she worked and how much she deserved the promotion. Six months later, she left the company for a position with the same title of director and a slightly higher salary. A year later, she left that organization and moved to another role. Four years later, she had moved a total of three times and was still no closer to the vice president title. The other colleague, on the other hand, stayed with the organization. One year later he was promoted to senior director. One year later a vice president retired and handpicked him as a replacement.

In the work place, we often forget the value of persistence. It's so easy to get discouraged when you do your best work and seem to be undervalued. Performance reviews are written about you and you wonder where your boss has been hiding all year long. Yet, if you observe those who are achieving the most in their careers, you will learn they are the ones who were persistent. Even when they received disappointing performance reviews, or when they were passed over for promotional opportunities, they never gave up.

In case you're not convinced, let's look at a few stories on persistence:

- Tim Ferriss sent his breakthrough New York Times bestselling book *4 Hour Workweek* to 25 publishers before one finally accepted it.

- Henry Ford's early businesses failed and left him broke 5 times before he founded Ford Motor Company.

- Thomas Edison's teachers said he was "too stupid to learn anything." He was fired from his first two jobs for being "non-productive." As an inventor, Edison made 1,000 unsuccessful attempts at inventing the light bulb.

- Rumor has it, Michael Jordan didn't make his high school's varsity basketball team when he first tried out because he simply was not good enough.

- Jim Carrey was booed off stage during his first comic stand-up at Yuk Yuk's Comedy Club in Toronto. Also, in 1980, he auditioned for Saturday Night Live and was rejected.

- Kathryn Stockett, the author of *The Help* was rejected by 60 literary agents before the book eventually was published and sold over ten million copies – and was turned into a movie.

- Colonel Sanders, founder of KFC, was 65 when he decided he would sell his fried chicken recipe. Sanders drove around the US knocking on doors, sleeping in his car and wearing his white suit. At age 90, in 1964, Sanders sold Kentucky Fried Chicken to a group of investors for $2 million.

- Steve Jobs, at age 30, was left devastated and depressed after being unceremoniously removed from the company he started.

- Oprah Winfrey was demoted from her job as news anchor because she "wasn't fit for television".

If you are following this book with the intention of applying the principles to grow your career, the first test as it relates to your PERSISTENCE will come when you begin to take a look at the very first principle. Will you work through and commit to growing your career, or will you give up and go back to doing what you were doing before? If you're a creative type like me and you struggle with persistence, here's a tip for you: set your end goals and stick to them. Keep the end goals at the forefront of your mind and don't do anything that's not in alignment with your end goals. Here are some questions to answer to get clear on your end goals:

- Where do you want to be in five years?
- What do you want to be doing in five years?
- In five years, what do you want to have?
- In five years, what do you want to give?

Once you've set your end goals, do everything you can to keep moving forward towards that end goal. It doesn't matter how slowly you go, just keep moving. With persistence comes success. Your next promotion is just on the other side of persistence.

Applying the Persistence Principle

- Get clear on your end goals by answering the above 5-year questions.

- Make a decision to keep moving forward and not quit.

- Review any area in the last 12 months that you have quit. Do you need to revisit these areas and make new commitments?

- Read autobiographies of great leaders who overcame challenges to stay motivated.

- Work through each of the Principles of Promotion determined to complete each assignment.

The Opportunity Principle

If somebody offers you an amazing opportunity but you are not sure you can do it, say yes – then learn how to do it later."

~ Richard Branson

One thing I know for sure is if you put each of these principles into place, and if you take the time to work on developing yourself, opportunities are certain to come your way. It will be a little daunting because one of the opportunities will be so huge it will blow your mind. Actually, it's going to scare the crap out of you. When it comes, without hesitation, take it. You've done all the hard work. At some point, you will receive a promotional opportunity. It may come in the form of a promotion in title. It may come in the form of a new role with another company. Your promotional opportunity might even come in the form of an entirely new career. Don't be afraid… well, you can be afraid. But go for it. As my mentor says often, "Jump and build your wings on the way down." The opportunity principle centered around your responsibility as you grow in your career. As you find yourself getting promoted, it's often easy to forget the people and strategies that helped you succeed. When you begin applying these principles and strategies for promotion, you should find yourself climbing the ladder of success. This principle is about what happens when opportunities arise. What happens after you get promoted? Here are five things to remember as you start to get promoted:

Stay humble – When you get promoted, it's easy to become arrogant. After all, you just got promoted. Resist this urge and remain humble. With every level of promotion also comes a slide down the food chain. When you get promoted, you go from the top of the food chain all the way down to the bottom of the food chain. It's like going from high school to college. Yes, you just graduated from the senior class, everyone applauded your efforts and celebrated you, then you go to college. You're a freshman all over again, learning your way around a much bigger school with all new people. It's the same thing when you get promoted. Stay humble as you learn your new role, new responsibilities and new people.

Remain teachable – Some lessons are best left untaught. Meaning, there are some lessons you can't learn in a classroom or in a book. There are some lessons you learn through watching others through what I call "teachable moments". When you finally receive that promotion, continue to have a teachable spirit. Life is all about lessons. The reason people become angry and bitter in their careers is because they have stopped being teachable. Being teachable means being open to learning from the lives and careers of others, even those who might have a lower title than you or those who might be younger than you. If you want to be more successful tomorrow, you must be teachable today. Keep your heart and attitude open to learning from others. If you are the smartest person in the room, get out of that room!

Know your lane – Don't forget the things you've learned that got you promoted. Continue to stay in your strengths. You may get promoted into a role that calls for you to lead others. But even though you're the "boss" it doesn't mean you are good at everything. Stay in your lane as a leader, honoring not only your strengths, but also the strengths, gifts and talents of others. Resist the urge to flex your leadership muscle in a way that diminishes the talents of others. Also, stay in your lane when it comes to your peer group. This is not the time to try to outshine your peers so you can be noticed. Once you get promoted, it's the time to be a great team player – the kind of team player who uses their gifts and talents to help others shine. Your time to shine will come again soon.

Start back at principle number one – You've done the hard work of getting promoted. Don't become complacent. Go back to the beginning and keep doing the things that got you promoted in the first place. Start with the mirror. What do you need to work on? Move from the mirror principle right into your brand. Your personal brand is now more important than ever. It's time to start rebuilding your brand at the new level. Don't stop there, keep going. Revisit each principle and remain consistent. You just might find your next promotion comes along just a little quicker and might even be easier this time.

Applying the Opportunity Principle

- When opportunities begin to come your way, remember to remain humble. Find a trusted accountability partner to help you keep your ego in check.

- Continue to learn and grow. Remain open to ideas from others.

- Surround yourself with people you can learn from, people who may have strengths that differ from yours.

The Success Principle

Being successful doesn't necessarily make you great. What makes you great is when you reach back and help somebody else become great.

~ Joel Osteen

The last principle is probably the easiest to forget, but it is the most important principle of them all. You are not really a success until you do one thing: **Reach back and pull someone else up with you.** With every level you reach, you have a responsibility to reach back and help someone else. You didn't get here on your own, someone helped you. Honor the legacy of great teachers by making a decision to help others. Find ways to reach back and pull someone else up. All great leaders leave a leadership legacy. Part of your legacy is to multiply. I'm going to let you in on a little secret. Lean in close, I'll whisper it, so the secret doesn't get out. Ready? "Contrary to what anybody says, there is enough for everybody." There can be more than one star at the company. There is enough money for everybody to have some. If you give away your knowledge, you will get more. Understand the message? Don't hoard your talent and your knowledge. Share it openly. Iron sharpens iron. But in order to become sharper, you have to come in contact with more iron. If iron comes in constant contact with wood, eventually the iron becomes dull. The true measure of a leader is his or her reproduction. Here are four ways to reproduce other great leaders to ensure your leadership legacy:

Mentor someone – You learned the mentor principle, now it's your turn to mentor someone else. Make a commitment to mentor at least one person outside of your immediate team for six to twelve months every year.

Be a sponsor – Become a sponsor for someone on your team – whether it be a peer or a direct report. Different from a mentor, being a sponsor means you make a conscious effort to help someone succeed. You champion for them. You ensure they are visible to the right people. Sponsor someone you know who is doing well and just needs the right person in their corner. Invite them to meetings and networking events, then introduce them to the right people.

Lead by example – Someone is always watching you. You are a role model whether you want to be one or not. There are people you may never know personally but they look up to you, admire you from afar. Always be a great example for others. Walk the walk of a great leader. Give others a great example to follow.

Be a visionary leader – Visionary leaders are leaders who look to the future and are always focused forward. Yes, they make mistakes, but they don't dwell on them. Visionary leaders are leaders who forgive quickly and hold no grudges. They set a vision for themselves and for those they lead. Be the kind of leader who is creative, passionate and continuously growing.

Applying the Success Principle

- Join a mentoring program where you can serve as a mentor to others within the organization.

- Become someone who sponsors others on the team. Make a list of three to five people whom you could sponsor and begin championing for them immediately.

- Behave as if someone important is watching your every move.

Conclusion

"The only thing separating you from your dreams is your ability to take action. The biggest bet you will ever place will be on you. Bet big!"

~Andrea Oden

Getting promoted can sometimes feel like a daunting task. To tell you the truth, sometimes it will take your focus on two or three principles and you'll find yourself getting promoted. Other times, you might work through all of the principles and not get a formal promotion, but an exciting project that could lead to promotion. Here's what I know: If you apply these principles, even a few of them, you will find yourself more marketable. You will find yourself growing into a much better leader. And isn't that what it's really all about? The world would be a much better place if everyone, every year, became a better leader.

Here are a few final pieces of advice to help you get promotion ready:

Take Ownership Of Your Career

Sometimes we are ambitious; we work hard, but we allow others to dictate our success, our growth. Your career is in your hands. The growth of your career rests with you and only you. I've had leaders in my career that I didn't see eye to eye with. In fact, I've worked for bosses that I flat out didn't like, and they didn't like me. However, these leaders did not control my career. These leaders had no power over my ability to get promoted. In fact, these leaders taught me some of my best lessons. They taught me lessons about myself and some serious lessons about leadership. I learned how to get along with anyone, not just those who I have things in common with. They taught me how to treat others when I got to a place of higher leadership. Always remember, your career is your own. Take ownership and never, ever give that power away.

Grab Some Friends And Start Principles Of Promotion Together

I encourage you to get a few likeminded friends and start working through the principles together. If you focus on one principle a month and hold each other accountable, sharing ideas and thoughts, you'd be surprised at your growth. Too often, we try to go on a journey alone and become frustrated and give up. Taking a journey with a friend is always better than going it alone.

Enjoy The Journey Of Your Career

We spend the majority of our hours at work. Learn to enjoy the journey. The real joy of this awesome career journey is that each step we take unfolds new ideas, new opportunities and new people. With each step we take on our career journey, we make new discoveries. We learn new things that make us better as people, better teammates and better leaders. With new knowledge comes new discoveries that keep us motivated to grow. Soon enough, we realize the destination, the end result, isn't really what we desire. What we actually desire isn't the title or the corner office. What we truly desired all along is growth, the growth we can only experience along the journey – and there is no finish line in this race. The journey is what's beautiful and satisfying. Where will your growth journey take you? For me, I've gone farther and done more things than I ever imagined. Thirty years ago, I was a word processor – that was my title. Today, I train leaders all over the United States. This has been an amazing journey that will still continue as long as I continue to grow. Take a step today. Make your personal growth part of your journey. Over time, you will look back and see how far you've come. Keep your mind open to new ideas, new opportunities and new people. Enjoy the journey. Live the dream!

Start Coaching With Me And My Team For Even Faster Results

Patrick Mouratoglou is the professional coach to Serena Williams, one of the greatest athletes of all times. Does she need tennis lessons? No, of course not. She needs a coach, someone who can help her see into the future. Serena doesn't need someone to tell her how to play the game of tennis. She needs a coach to help her see how to get beyond her current level and onto the next level. She needs someone to advise her on next steps. She needs someone to talk challenges over with. She needs someone to help put strategies in place to help her get to the next level of her game. That's what you need. You need a coach who can guide you, correct your technique and identify areas of improvement. That's what my team does. We provide support as you grow in your career.

To learn more about how you can be part of our coaching experience, visiting my website:

https:\\www.andreaoden.com

Principles of Promotion and other career advice is available from Andrea Oden via podcast, Monday Evening Mentor. Download Monday Evening Mentor with Andrea Oden and listen to career advice on your favorite device or by subscribing today at

https://www.stitcher.com/podcast/monday-evening-mentor

http://mondayeveningmentor.blubrry.net/

About Andrea Oden

An award-winning speaker, author, coach and a seasoned Senior Human Resources Professional, Andrea Oden engages and challenges today's leaders with her bold and audacious approach to leadership. She is an enthusiastic leadership partner who has shaped high performing sales and customer service cultures at Fortune 500 and major growth brands.

As a certified John Maxwell Leadership Development Coach, Andrea uses a unique blend of communication skills, employee relations savvy and executive level coaching designed to empower leaders and strengthen any business at its core. She is a dynamo speaker who can engage any team, always leaving her audience wanting more.

Andrea is also the host of the 2018 People's Choice Award nominated podcast, Monday Evening Mentor. Andrea Oden is leaving an undeniable mark on the leadership and development industry, daily.

Andrea lives in a Michigan Suburb with her family but calls Chicago home.

Made in the USA
Columbia, SC
19 September 2019